The Life of a SUNFLOWER

Clare Hibbert

www.raintreepublishers.co.uk
Visit our website to find out more information about **Raintree** books.

To order:
☎ Phone 44 (0) 1865 888112
🖹 Send a fax to 44 (0) 1865 314091
💻 Visit the Raintree Bookshop at **www.raintreepublishers.co.uk** to browse our catalogue and order online.

First published in Great Britain by Raintree, Halley Court, Jordan Hill, Oxford OX2 8EJ, part of Harcourt Education.
Raintree is a registered trademark of Harcourt Education Ltd.

Editorial: Nick Hunter and Catherine Clarke
Design: Michelle Lisseter and Tipani Design
   (www.tipani.co.uk)
Illustration: Tony Jones, Art Construction
Picture Research: Maria Joannou and Elaine Willis
Production: Jonathan Smith

Originated by Dot Gradations Ltd
Printed and bound in China by South China Printing Company

ISBN 1 844 43305 6
08 07 06 05 04
10 9 8 7 6 5 4 3 2 1

British Library Cataloguing in Publication Data
Hibbert, Clare
The Life of a Sunflower. – (Life Cycles)
571.8'2399
A full catalogue record for this book is available from the British Library.

Acknowledgements
The publishers would like to thank the following for permission to reproduce photographs:
A–Z Botanical Collection p. **19**; Corbis p. **23**; FLPA pp. **4** (J. C. Allen), **20** (Chris Demetriou), **22** (S. Maslowski), **24** (Chris Demetriou), **26** (Roger Tidman); Garden and Wildlife Matters p. **5**; Getty Images pp. **11** (Imagebank), **13** (Stone); Holt Studios pp. **9** (Nigel Cattlin), **12** (Nigel Cattlin), **15**, **17**; National Sunflower Association pp. **10**, **14**, **16**, **18**, **25**, **27**, **29**; Nature Picture Library (Fabio Liverani) p. **28**; Oxford Scientific Films (Mantis Wildlife Films) p. **21**; Paul Beard Photo Library p. **8**.

Cover photograph of a sunflower head, reproduced with permission of Science Photo Library (John Mead).

The publishers would like to thank Janet Stott for her assistance in the preparation of this book.

Every effort has been made to contact copyright holders of any material reproduced in this book. Any omissions will be rectified in subsequent printings if notice is given to the publishers.

The paper used to print this book comes from sustainable resources.

Contents

Any words appearing in bold, **like this**, are explained in the Glossary.

The sunflower

Sunflowers are beautiful plants that have big, bright flower heads. Gardeners plant them to brighten up their flowerbeds. Many are grown for their **seeds**. The seeds can be pressed to make oil for cooking or used in snack foods and bird feed. Sunflowers are also grown to sell in flower shops. Some sunflowers grow in the wild.

Have you ever seen an enormous field of yellow sunflowers like this one?

Growing up

Just as you grow bigger year by year, the sunflower grows and changes. All the sunflower's changes happen between spring and autumn of a single year – and in that short time it can grow taller than you! The different stages of the sunflower's life make up its **life cycle**. There are several types of sunflower, but they all share the same basic life cycle.

Sunflowers are popular with gardeners of all ages, because they are so easy to grow.

Where in the world?

Sunflowers first grew as wildflowers in North America. Today they are grown as **crops** by farmers all over the world. Russia is the country that grows the most sunflowers.

A sunflower's life

The sunflower begins its life as a **seed** that is planted in the ground in spring. The seed quickly puts out **roots** and a **shoot**. It also grows leaves. The sunflower grows fast, soon reaching a height of about 2 metres or more – that is much taller than you.

By the time it is six weeks old, the plant's huge flower head is opening out. The flower head is surrounded by petals. The centre of the flower head is made up of lots of miniature flowers called **florets**.

Going to seed

Each miniature flower can swell into a seed. If the sunflower is being grown for its seeds the farmer will harvest it when it is around sixteen weeks old. Some plants are missed. These die back and slowly rot. The remains of the plants add extra **nutrients** to the soil.

Sunflower seeds are planted in spring.

After about a week, the plant puts out its first leaves.

At four weeks old, the plant is tall and leafy.

At six weeks old, the flower **bud** can be seen.

The sunflower blooms at around eight or nine weeks old.

At sixteen weeks old, the seeds are ripe.

This diagram shows the **life cycle** of a sunflower, from seed to flower.

Planting the seed

In spring, the sunflower **seed** is planted in the warm, damp soil. It is planted about 4 centimetres below the surface. If it is planted too near to the surface, rains might wash away its covering of soil or even the seed itself. If the seed is planted any deeper, the surface will be too far away for the plant's **shoot** to reach the sunlight.

A sunflower seed is planted by pushing it into some damp soil.

Spring shoots

The warmth and water in the soil make the seed burst into life. This is called **germination**. Seeds need warmth and water to germinate but not light. After a few days, the **husk** or outer casing of the seed splits. A white and green shoot comes out, pointing up, and hairy **roots**, spreading down. The roots suck **nutrients** and water from the soil. These things help the sunflower plant to grow.

Soil story

Soil contains some bits of broken rock, but mostly it is made from the rotting remains of dead animals and, especially, plants. Underground creatures, such as worms, help to make the soil rich and crumbly.

This sunflower seed was planted 3 days ago. Its shoot is nearly at the surface and its roots are pushing down into the soil.

First leaves

The **shoot** from the sunflower **seed** travels up to the surface towards the light. Soon, it pokes out of the ground. The shoot keeps climbing. When it is about a week old, the plant grows its first pair of leaves. Over the next week, more leaves follow.

Plant food

The sunflower's first pair of leaves are different to the later ones. Their shape is more rounded.

The leaves are covered with fine hairs that help to stop water escaping. They also have tiny holes in their surfaces. The holes take in gases from the air. The leaves use the gases to help make food for the plant. They mix the gases with the sunlight that they soak up each day, and the water that reaches them from the **roots**.

Together, the air, light and water are used to make special sugars. This process is called photosynthesis. The sugars feed the whole plant. They help it to grow more leaves and, later, to make a giant flower head.

Underneath the soil, the plant puts out a tangle of roots.

Growing up

For the first four weeks, the sunflower battles for survival. It needs sunlight, water and **nutrients** from the soil. The problem is, all plants need these things. Weeds, such as wild mustard, grow among the sunflowers. They try to take all the light, water and nutrients.

These sunflower plants are about two weeks old. They are already much bigger than the nearby weeds.

Two's a crowd

The sunflower spreads out its **roots**, so that it can suck up more water and nutrients than the weeds. It grows taller and puts out bigger leaves so that no weeds can block out its sunlight. The sunflower's leaves soon crowd out most of the weeds. When the weeds cannot reach the sunlight, they wilt and die.

One way to get rid of weeds is to spray them with weedkiller. This farmer is spraying crops from a special aeroplane.

Weed killers

Farmers and gardeners who grow sunflowers help fight the weeds. They turn the soil to bury the weeds. Farmers do this using tractors that drag a special soil-turning tool, called a **harrow**. Gardeners use a hand tool, such as a hoe.

Strong and sturdy

As the sunflower grows taller, it is also busy beneath the soil. It puts out many **roots**. The roots spread out and push down. Some grow down so deep that they are longer than the plant's stem. All these roots hold the plant firmly in the soil. They keep it steady, even when the weather is windy.

By the time they are a month old, the sunflowers are about 1 metre tall with thick, strong stems.

Sunshade

While the roots are growing deeper into the ground, the plant's stem keeps on growing straight up towards the light. It puts out leaves from the tip of its stem. The leaves spread out to make a **canopy**. They shelter the ground from the hot summer sun. This helps the roots in the ground to stay cool.

Leaf eaters

Have you ever seen a leaf with a hole in it? Sunflower leaves get nibbled by field slugs, snails and thistle caterpillars. They are also the favourite food of the sunflower beetle. Both the adult beetles and their **grubs** munch through the leaves.

Big bud

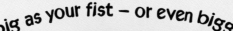

When the plant is about six weeks old, there is a change. By now the plant can be around 2 metres tall or more. Its stem is thicker than your thumb. The growing **shoot** stops making leaves. It has enough leaves. It is time to put out the flower head.

A sunflower bud can be as big as your fist – or even bigger!

Small package

A fat flower **bud** swells at the tip of the plant. It has special green outer petals, called **bracts**. These protect the delicate yellow petals inside the bud. The flower bud contains everything that will make the sunflower's great big flower head. It is all packed inside, very tightly.

Stem feeders

The sunflower needs a sturdy stem to support its giant flower head. Some insects eat away at the stem and weaken it. They include sunflower moth caterpillars, sunflower maggots and sunflower stem weevils (shown in this photograph). Even the stem's bristly hairs cannot stop these pests.

In bloom

Slowly, the flower head **bud** gets fatter. Then the petals start to open out. When they are open, the flower head has a circle of bright, yellow petals surrounding a bumpy brown centre.

The **bracts** curl back and the flower begins to open. Sunflowers that are going to be sold as cut flowers are harvested just as the petals open out.

Sunflower surprise

The sunflower looks as if it is one single giant flower – but look again! Each of the tiny bumps in the centre of the flower head is a miniature flower, called a **floret**. In total, there can be as many as 1000 florets on the flower head. Now that the flower head is blooming, the florets begin to open, one by one.

Following the Sun

Many sunflowers are able to do something very special. In the morning they face east, towards the rising Sun. As the Sun moves across the sky, the stem turns to follow it. The flower heads always point towards the light of the Sun. Sunflowers get their name because they are the only plants able to do this.

Pollen

Each tiny **floret** in the centre of a sunflower has both male and female parts. Different male and female parts need to come together so that the florets can produce **seeds**.

All of the tiny bumps in the middle of the sunflower head are florets.

Landing platform

The floret has male parts called **stamens**. At the end of each stamen are grains of yellow **pollen**. To honey bees, pollen is like gold dust! They need the pollen in order to survive. The bright yellow colour of the flowers helps the bees find the pollen. They zoom in and land on the flower head. As well as the pollen, the florets have sweet **nectar** for the bees to collect.

Making honey

Honey bees collect nectar and pollen to make honey. Honey feeds all the adult bees in the hive. Pollen is also used to make bee bread. This is special food for the baby bee **grubs**. It is made by mixing pollen grains, honey and juices bees spit out of their mouths. Yum!

Swelling seeds

Each time a honey bee visits a sunflower **floret**, grains of **pollen** stick to its furry body. At the next floret, some of the pollen grains rub off. Hopefully, they rub on to the female part of a floret. This process is called **pollination**. This happens a lot, because each bee is busy visiting as many flowers as possible.

The bee pollinates the florets. It carries pollen that has stuck to its body from one floret to another.

Fertilization

The floret's female part is called the **carpel**. Something amazing happens when pollen from a different floret touches the tip of the carpel, called the stigma. The pollen starts to move down the stigma inside the floret. Right in the centre is the floret's **ovary**. This is where the floret stores its egg, called an **ovule**.

When the pollen joins with the ovule, it can grow into a **seed**. This process is called **fertilization**. After fertilization, the ovule starts to swell.

On this sunflower, the outer florets are fertilized. You can see the dark tips of the seeds.

Fading flower

The sunflower's bright yellow petals caught the attention of honey bees. Now that the **florets** have been **pollinated**, the sunflower does not need to attract bees any more. The petals crumple and turn brown. Soon, they fall off. The plant's green leaves wilt. They also start to turn yellow and brown.

At this stage in its **life cycle**, the sunflower may look like it is dying but it is very much alive. It is putting all its effort into making seeds.

Circle of seeds

At the top of the plant's stem, the heavy
flower head droops in the summer heat.
The florets have all withered.
In the place of each
floret, there is a dark,
growing **seed**.

Seed tunnellers

Have you ever eaten sunflower
seeds? They give your body
lots of energy. Insects,
especially sunflower seed
weevils, like to eat the seeds
too. The seeds give the
insects energy to grow.

Seed dispersal

Now the sunflower plant is sixteen weeks old. Its **seeds** have ripened in the sunshine. Some of the seeds are eaten by hungry birds. Seed-eating birds have short, stocky beaks for cracking open the seeds. Sometimes, they fly away from the plant with a seed in their beak and then drop the seed. The way that birds carry seeds to a new place to grow is called seed dispersal.

A great tit pecks at the seeds on this flower head.

Mouse hoards

Seeds that fall to the ground near the plant can be gathered up by field mice and voles. Some will be eaten, but others are buried in secret underground stores. If the mice forget where they put them, some of these seeds might be able to grow into new plants next spring.

Harvest

Farmers harvest their sunflowers for the ripe seeds. They drive a big machine, called a combine harvester, through the field. This cuts the sunflower stems and beats out the seeds, which are collected in the harvester.

Seeds for all

Sunflowers are annuals. That means that in one year's growing season they produce their **seeds** and die. One sunflower produces hundreds of sunflower seeds. Each of these might be able to grow into a whole new sunflower plant. Sometimes people collect seeds for planting. They store the seeds over the winter and then plant them in the spring. In the wild, the sunflower seeds rest in the ground over winter. Some are eaten, but plenty survive to become new sunflowers.

Harvested sunflower seeds end up in many places – including this pet guinea pig's tummy!

New life

Seeds need warmth and moisture to burst into life, or **germinate**. In spring, when the conditions are right, they start to grow. They put out **roots** and **shoots**, and the **life cycle** begins all over again.

Where the harvested seeds go

Most harvested seeds are pressed, or squashed very hard, for their oil. They make sunflower oil and margarine. Some are used in animal feed mixes. People eat sunflower seeds, too. They make a tasty, healthy snack.

At this factory, sunflower seeds are roasted for eating.

Find out for yourself

The best way to find out more about the **life cycle** of a sunflower is to watch it happen with your own eyes. You can plant one in the garden, or in a plant pot on a balcony.

Books to read

Fun with Gardening: 50 Great Projects Kids Can Plant Themselves Clare Bradley (Southwater, 2000)
How things grow: From Seed to Sunflower Sally Morgan (Belitha Press, 2002)

Using the Internet

Explore the Internet to find out more about sunflowers. Websites can change, and if some of the links below no longer work, don't worry. Use a search engine, such as www.yahooligans.com, and type in keywords such as 'sunflower', 'life cycle' and '**pollinate**'.

Websites

http://www.cyberspaceag.com/sunflowersun.html
Find out some fun facts about sunflowers, including tips on how to grow them.
http://www.enchantedlearning.com/themes/flowers.shtml
Have a go at these activities, and find facts as well as printouts to colour in.

Disclaimer
All the Internet addresses (URLs) given in this book were valid at the time of going to press. However, due to the dynamic nature of the Internet, some addresses may have changed, or sites may have ceased to exist since publication. While the author and publishers regret any inconvenience this may cause readers, no responsibility for any such changes can be accepted by either the author or the publishers.

Glossary

bract leafy, green petal that protects a flower bud

bud tightly-packed plant shoot that may open out into a leaf or flower

canopy layer or covering of plants

carpel female part of the flower, made up of the stigma, style and ovary

crop plant that farmers grow

fertilization when male and female parts join together to create a new living thing, such as an animal or plant

floret single, tiny flower that grows alongside many other tiny flowers. Together, the florets make up one big flower head.

germination when a seed begins to grow, putting out shoots

grub young insect that looks nothing like its parent

harrow tool used to turn over soil and get rid of any weeds

husk thin shell that protects a seed. The husks of sunflower seeds are usually plain black, or striped black and white.

life cycle all the different stages in the life of a living thing, such as an animal or plant

nectar sugary food that flowers produce to attract pollinating insects, such as honey bees

nutrients something that feeds a living thing. Nutrients or goodness in soil feed plants.

ovary female part of the flower, containing the flower's ovules

ovule female cells, or eggs, that can grow into a seed when they have joined together with pollen

pollen powdery grains containing the male cells of a flower

pollination when male pollen from one flower joins with a female egg from another flower, so that a seed can start to grow

root part of a plant that pushes down into the soil. Its job is to suck up water and to steady the plant.

seed small package produced by a plant that contains the beginnings of a new plant inside it

shoot stem-like growth that comes out of a seed once it has germinated

stamen male part of the flower. Its stalk is called the filament and the end, which carries pollen, is called the anther.

Index

Titles in the *Life Cycles* series include:

Hardback   1 844 43300 5

Hardback   1 844 43301 3

Hardback   1 844 43302 1

Hardback   1 844 43303 X

Hardback   1 844 43304 8

Hardback   1 844 43305 6

Find out about the other titles in this series on our website www.raintreepublishers.co.uk